A CLEAR AND PRESENT DANGER

a matter of personal freedom and economic prosperity

I0439989

Patrick Thomas

ISBN: 1490314121
ISBN-13: 978-1490314129

DEDICATION

To my wife Pam for her patience, encouragement, and enthusiastic proof reading

Table of Contents

Preface

The flag of The United States of America flies above my home 24 hours a day, 365 days a year. Why don't I take it down at night? I used to, but a fort under siege never lowers its flag. And we are all under siege, both from without and within—including by our Federal Government

Wake up America! This is no time to be giving the Administration the benefit of the doubt; we are in trouble.

I'm not a politician nor am I an academic. I'm an American with a reasonably good education (BA in economics and political science 1960) who has worked for many different companies in several industries for more than fifty years.

I have followed national politics for years. I passed the three quarter century mark more than a year ago. I remember what I was doing when Pearl Harbor was attacked and on VE and VJ days.

I remember the concerns of nuclear annihilation that swept the country during the cold war. I sweated my National Guard unit being called to war during the Berlin and the Cuban missile crises.

And I have never been as concerned as I am now.

In all of those other times, the United States was a strong nation because of the strength of its citizens. The U. S. population held to a strong work ethic and moral code. Now, the ruling plurality dismisses individual achievement and traditional morality in favor of government handouts and being careful to not offend minorities—even if this means the destruction of the majority will. And the destruction of the majority's culture and rights.

We elected a president with little experience, and about whom we knew next to nothing hoping for a "...change we could believe in." We got the slowest financial recovery in the history of our nation (it's still going and shows signs of getting worse before it gets better), a tremendous increase in national debt, an almost total loss of respect for our government in the international community, and a growing list of federal government scandals.

So what did we do about it? We reelected him for a second term. This is the scary part. Have enough voters gotten tied into the gravy train to always swing the vote in favor of handouts?

The 2012 elections were the last really good chance to save things without having to go through a major crash and bitter recovery. Wake up, people! This is not the time for balanced discussion. The verdict is in on the Obama administration, and that verdict is failure. Not to mention a very strong red flag: DANGER.

A Clear and Present Danger.

Summary

We are under siege. The United States of America is under siege from several fronts:

We are under siege by militant Islamists (9/11, Iraq and Afghanistan, along with the various foreign and domestic terrorist attacks, are just parts of this). They are not attacking us because we are free and prosperous, nor because we have troops in Asia, nor because we have not closed Guantanamo. They are attacking us because we are infidels. "Islam by the sword."

We are at war with drug cartels on our southern border. They have outposts in U.S. Territory. We have been invaded by the drug cartels.

Our southern border is undefended; we have been overrun by illegal immigrants.

Our own government is attempting to destroy our nation as we know it. The current federal government is the most left leaning in our history. It is trying to remake our country to match Europe—just as the European economy is failing from the weight of their governments.

The Obama administration is totally ignoring the Constitution and establishing new "laws" through executive orders coming out of the

White House and rulings by the massive number of federal agencies created or enlarged by the "Imperial Presidency".

Where are we now?

Nearly half way through the slowest economic recovery in U.S. history (or perhaps the end of recovery and the start of the next downturn), saddled with useless laws and restrictions that hamper business growth, losing two wars (and having lost the international respect we once had), with an open southern border, and with an administration that enforces the law very selectively, and is increasingly swamped with scandals which it attempts to cover up by stonewalling: that's where we are!

What can we do? In the short term, we have to pull out of the ditch and stop the runaway pull to the left. In the long term, we have to make corrections to our government (largely returns to the original Constitutional principles) to avoid future runaways (*to either the left or the right*).

And vote! Voting is an obligation as well as a right.

To the person who just said, "I'm tired of voting for the lesser of evils"; so am I, but if you don't vote, you cast a de facto vote for the *greater* evil.

We Are Under Siege

The United States of America is under siege from several fronts:

1. We are under siege by militant Islamists.

2. National defense begins at the border.

3. We have been invaded by illegal immigrants.

4. Our own government is attempting to destroy our nation as we know it.

We Are Under Siege By Militant Islamists.

Islam is two things:

1. A religion

2. A political movement

Islam The Religion

Islam is a monotheistic faith closely related to Judaism and Christianity. In fact, it shares with them many of the same prophets, including Abraham, Moses, and with Christianity, Jesus.

Muslims believe that Islam is the primordial faith that was revealed at many times and places, including through Abraham, Moses and Jesus, before being presented in its final form through Muhammad.

According to Islamic tradition, God sent messengers to every nation before finally sending Muhammad to transmit the message of the Qur'an, the holy book considered by Islam to be universal.

Islamic tradition holds that previous Islamic holy books, the Torah given to Moses, the Psalms given to David, and the Gospel given to Jesus, were for a particular time and location, and were superseded by Muhammad and the universal Qur'an.

I knew many Muslims when I lived in Afghanistan in 1950 and had religious discussions with many of them when I was in college. It always seemed to me that the only difficulty of coexistence with them was the insistence on Sharia law.

Islam The Political Movement

We are not at war with the Islamic religion, but we are at war with a group of Islamic extremists intent on establishing a world wide Caliphate, an Islamic state led by a supreme religious as well as political leader, and governed in accordance with Sharia law.

We are under siege by militant Islamists (9/11, Iraq and Afghanistan, along with the various foreign and domestic terrorist attacks, are just parts of this). They are not attacking us because we are free and prosperous, nor because we have troops in Asia, nor because we have not closed Guantanamo. They are attacking us because we are infidels. "Islam by the sword."

National Defense Begins At The Border

We are at war with drug cartels on our southern border. They have outposts in U.S. Territory. We have been invaded.

We are not at war with Mexico—not yet. The U.S. And Mexico both share a common enemy, the drug cartels. But if the major cartels either unite rather than fight each other, or one wins and becomes dominant, we will be—because the drug cartels will take over the government of Mexico.

The current administration has not only refused to control the border, it has strongly fought any attempts that the border states have made to protect their citizens using their police powers, claiming that the Constitution gives all authority for controlling borders to the Federal Government.

Let's look at that.

Article 1, Section 8 of the Constitution calls for the Federal Government:

...To establish a uniform Rule of Naturalization...throughout the United States...

Article IV, Section 4 requires:

The United States...shall protect each of them (each state) against Invasion;

Article. II, Section 3 requires that:

... he (the President) shall take Care that the Laws be faithfully executed...

Article 1 Section 10 states:

No State shall... engage in War, unless actually invaded, or in such imminent Danger as will not admit of delay.

To summarize:

Article 1, Section 8 says that states cannot pass their own rules of naturalization. This is preempted by the Federal Government.

Article IV, Section 4 requires the Federal Government to protect each state against invasion.

Article II, Section 3 requires the President to see that *all* laws be enforced.

Article 1, Section 10 simply says that, for instance, Arizona can't invade Mexico no matter how angry they get about illegal aliens and drug trafficking.

When you add the **10ᵗʰ Amendment:**

"The powers not delegated to the United States by the Constitution, nor prohibited by it to the States, are reserved to the States respectively, or to the people".

And also taking into account the well established recognition of the states' authority to use their police powers to maintain order, it would seem that the feds are the ones who are deficient.

They have not, "protected each of them against invasion."

And as far as the President taking care, "that the laws be faithfully executed"? In this and other matters (most other matters?) the current Justice Department (led by Eric Holder) is *very selective* as to which laws to enforce and which to not enforce and when to enforce them.

We Have Been Invaded By Illegal Immigrants

How many illegal immigrants are living in the United States?

Estimates vary, but the most common estimate is 15 to 20 million. Researchers estimate that the number of immigrants sneaking across the border every year averages more than 300,000.

The Pew Research Center's latest estimate of the number of illegal aliens residing in the United States—11.7 million as of March 2012—was less than most estimates, but it still exceeds the approximately 11.46 million people whom the Bureau of Labor Statistics says were unemployed in the average month of 2013.

Census Bureau data shows that most U.S. families headed by illegal immigrants use taxpayer-funded welfare programs on behalf of their American-born children who get automatic citizenship. Food assistance and Medicaid are the programs most commonly used by illegal immigrants, mainly on behalf of their American-born children.

By contrast, legal immigrant households take advantage of every available welfare program, with welfare use tending to be high for both new arrivals and established residents.

What does this say for amnesty? It would result in even greater tax payer burdens.

About amnesty. Ronald Reagan approved what he thought would be a limited amnesty in return for increased border security. What he got was major amnesty, no improvement in border security, and an increase in the rate of illegal immigration.

Now, the Obama administration is pushing for "comprehensive immigration reform" (read amnesty with a path to citizenship). Why?

This would lead to many more low income voters dependent on government assistance (who would most likely vote democrat; vote for the welfare state). Could this be the reason?

Our Own Government Is Attempting To Destroy Our Nation As We Know It

Democrats blame a lot of their problems on a "Vast right-wing conspiracy." Political commentators speak of the far left and the far right in politics. Interestingly enough, if you go far enough left, or far enough right you meet. It's called tyranny. (Think left Stalin or Mao, right Adolf Hitler).

It would seem that there is a rather broad road that's safe to travel politically. How do you stay on it? Do you elect only candidates dedicated to staying on that road? Good luck in finding them.

No, some politicians will always continually pull left and some will always continually pull right. The government then goes down the road veering left and right and, hopefully, staying on the highway. The problem comes when the pull gets too steady in one direction for too long a time and the government runs off the road and bogs down.

This is the current condition of the United States federal government. It has gone so far to the left that we're in a ditch. Didn't Margaret Thatcher say that socialism works until you run out of someone else's money?

Well we have, and are borrowing recklessly and creating additional cash with nothing behind it to fund more government spending to shore up an artificial recovery (which is visible only on Wall Street—can anyone say "Stock Market bubble"?).

And the Government is attempting to destroy our National Traditions. More on that below.

How Are The External Battles Going?

Afghanistan

I remember as a senior in high school having completed all the questions but one in a current events test I was taking. That question required listing six of the nations belonging to the United Nations. I was stymied at five.

When I gave up and turned the test in, The instructor broke out laughing. "You lived there."

"I included Canada."

"The other foreign country you lived in."

"Afghanistan? It's not even a government."

I was right. In 1951 Afghanistan was culturally but not politically a nation. The people spoke of being Afghans, but even in the big southern city of Kandahar the Afghan government was referred to as, "The Kabul government".

In Kajakai, the village that bordered the construction camp where I celebrated my 13th birthday, the tribal leader was more concerned with the tribe across the Helmand River than he was the Kabul government. As long as he paid his taxes, the King left him alone.

Although the mud walled village across the Helmand was so distant that it was easily spotted only at night when the lamps were lighted, the Kajakai residents considered it unsafe to be caught on the other side of the river after dark.

Kajakai's tribal leader occasionally made a formal visit to the construction site riding in on a magnificent gold chestnut stallion accompanied by his retinue on slightly lesser but still impressive steeds, and a free running young filly obviously the daughter of his stallion.

They would ride by the riverbed rock and mortar houses, where the American construction crew families lived, on their way into camp in their colorful clothing and equipment, contrasting sharply with the much drabber horse and camel riders that we usually saw.

I never met Kajakai's leader, but he heard of my 13 year old love of horses and gave me (loaned while I was there) that filly.

Then there was the one visit by the leader of the village across the Helmand.

He was reported to hold the King of Afghanistan in disdain claiming that he was the rightful King of Afghanistan. He paid no taxes having, according to the story, slaughtered an army tax collection detail. The king then sent one of the two airplanes in the Afghan air force to bomb the village. They dropped a bomb, it missed, and that was the end of the matter. (Again, this is according to the generally accepted story among the Afghans).

When the visit was scheduled, no one from Kajakai was in sight by sundown. At dusk, harness bells sounded, and a nearly white racing camel tore by at full speed with two or three lesser (but still above average) camels struggling to keep up.

They had apparently crossed the Helmand above and passed in front of the village of Kajakai; four or five men with rifles scorning a full village of armed men. Such is the value of reputation.

All of the cultural nation of Afghanistan was full of similar tribal standoffs. The King was an absolute monarch, but only in Kabul. His authority declined with distance from the capital.

From what I have read written by those with current experience in Afghanistan, Karzai is in an even lesser situation than the King was. He is not an absolute monarch. He does have a much more modern army, but civilization has lessened the distance between the capital at Kabul and the tribal leaders, who also are better equipped militarily. And of course the group of Islamic extremists intent on establishing a world wide Caliphate, an Islamic state led by a supreme religious as well as political leader, did not exist as a problem for the King.

Our nation has invested a tremendous amount of expense and lives lost in Afghanistan. Should we have? Nothing can be done about that now, we did. If we surrender now (which is what the Obama administration is essentially doing) we add to the reputation that, "You can't trust The United States. They'll elect a new government and back out."

However, electing a new government wasn't necessary in this case. Remember how Obama touted Afghanistan as the "good" war and Iraq as the "bad" (read "...we can blame this one on Bush") war?

As could be seen in the example that I made above of the few camel riders disdainfully traveling past a whole village of their enemies, reputation is a powerful thing. It works both ways. After backing off multiple red lines, I doubt if Obama could lead strongly if he tried.

What should we do about Afghanistan? I don't know. What we must do is change the runaway direction of our government. That is the topic of a later chapter.

Iraq

I have no personal insight into Iraq. The only times I was there were two sleepy periods of long waits at the Baghdad airport between flights going to and returning from Afghanistan.

But from what I understand, Iraq is like Afghanistan in being comprised of many less than friendly entities, having been created as a country by the allies at the end of World War II to offset Iran as a military force.

Prior to the U.S. Invasion, the iron hand of Saddam Hussein's dictatorship held the conflicting factions together, but when Hussein's army invaded and annexed Kuwait, this created a crisis beyond the invasion itself.

Since the end of WW II, any degree of peace that existed resulted from the standoff between the two super powers, the United States and the Union of Soviet Socialist Republics. With the fall of the USSR, a vacuum was created. Saddam Hussein was the first to test the changed climate. If he achieved success, other countries covetous of their neighbors—and there are many—would follow suit.

The recognition of this crisis can be seen by the size (34 nations) of the coalition formed. The feared Iraqi Republican Guard was soundly defeated and all of the invading troops were driven back to Iraq in relatively short order.

When the Iraqi forces broke and retreated home, chastened but not horribly diminished in power, the coalition ceased.

Later, concerns of Saddam Hussein's accumulation of weapons of mass destruction resulted in the invasion of Iraq and the start of the Iraq war. Again the defeat of the Iraq army was relatively easy and many In Iraq welcomed being freed from Hussein.

But then the "nation building" effort started with the U.S. attempting to establish a democratic government in Iraq. The response of the less than friendly entities was something like: "You freed us from that tyrant Hussein. Thank you. Now get out of here and let us kill each other." When we didn't, that was the real start of the Iraq war.

The anticipated chemical weapons of mass destruction were not found, leading to a lot of, "I always said there weren't any," from politicians although there had been almost universal agreement that they were there. Ah politics, such 2020 hind-sights.

As with Afghanistan, much money was spent and many lives lost. Perhaps we shouldn't have, perhaps we should, but we did. No changing that now.

What should we do about Iraq? I don't know. What we must do is change the runaway direction of our government. That is the topic of a later chapter.

Our Southern Border

More is coming across our southern border than illegal immigrants looking for work. The drug cartels are not only smuggling drugs into the U.S. across our southern border, they have invaded and set up surveillance outposts on U.S. Soil to track law enforcement efforts and monitor smugglers around them. We have been invaded.

What is our government's answer? Declare certain areas of our country as unsafe and fight state efforts to quell the problems.

Jihad

How is the battle against the group of Islamic extremists intent on establishing a world wide Caliphate, an Islamic state led by a supreme religious as well as political leader, and governed in accordance with Sharia law?

According to Obama, that was won before the last election. Al Qaeda is broken and in retreat. The war on terror has been won. All that was needed to achieve this was to redefine all terror attacks as protests that got out of hand or work place violence. Oh yes, there was one case of "domestic violence" when scores of peaceful protestors confronted the BLM invasion of Nevada. More on that later.

However, if you believe intelligence reports, Al Qaeda has enlarged its influence in territory and control of people in the Middle East and in Africa.

Of course when you consider the recent large apparently unworried outdoor Al Qaeda gathering in Yemen, perhaps they agree that the war on terror is over and that they've won.

The Obama Administration

When I studied political science in college, there were many different opinions on who had been the best President of the United States, but there was general agreement on who had been the most inept: Ulysses Grant, a great General Officer but a poor President.

Then Jimmy Carter came along and at least rivaled President Grant. President Carter was and is a good, moral man but he was an inept President.

President Barack Obama, based on his record to date, is certainly in the running for the title of most inept President that the United States has ever had, but he is without question the most dangerous President that the United States has ever had.

Most Inept

When Barack Obama became President for his first term, the United States was plagued with a serious recession—business failures and a high level of unemployment—and wars: in Iraq, Afghanistan, on our southern border, and the ongoing war on terror.

After the completion of his first term and well into the second: we are in the process of surrendering in Iraq and Afghanistan, and the southern border is probably less secure, but the war on terror has been won according to Obama. All he had to do to achieve this was redefine all terror attacks as protests that got out of hand or work place violence.

And the economy? The stock market has recovered due to government bailouts and massive spending intended to jump start private sector business growth. But the private sector hasn't jumped. The national debt has doubled and the economy is dependent on continuation of massive government spending, an outlay that we cannot afford. The government is broke.

And unemployment, real unemployment including those who have given up looking for work, is at least as high as when he took office.

This is the slowest and most expensive recovery from a recession in our nation's history.

President Obama's answer: more spending of the same sort only increase taxes on the wealthy to lessen the deficit (funny how the definition of wealthy keeps getting lower and lower; pretty soon it will include everyone not on welfare).

Tax increases to stimulate the private sector economy? That will never work in this reality. (Maybe in another dimension where rabbits rule, the sky is made of water, and the ocean of air).

Liberal economists point to how government deficit spending brought us out of the Great Depression, slowly at first and then with the accelerated spending on the 2nd World War effort the economy surged.

But what is really to be learned from this?

First, although the initial recovery efforts were inefficient (think, "Shovel Leaners"), the dollars *were* employing people to do useful things. When the war effort began, the nation was scared (and patriotic). No more shovel leaning. Production was intense and unemployment was almost nonexistent.

The predicted terrible post war recession did not happen because the public's demand for goods took over from the war effort.

So how is the current government spending different? It's not resulting in private economy job creation because it isn't producing anything.

It is:

1. Expanding the size of the federal government

2. Supporting failing projects (think Solyndra)

3. Increasing welfare

And it is accompanied by increasing the difficulty of doing business with laws, executive orders, EPA regulations, and the like. The most onerous of these being the requirements of Obamacare, together with the uncertainty of what these requirements will be.

Immediately after Obama won reelection, his house of cards began to fall apart. Problems that would probably have cost him the election had they come out earlier began to emerge—along with evidence that they had been kept under cover with a series of cover ups.

These scandals include:

1. The IRS attack against conservative political groups

2. The NSA "Big Brother" spying on the American public

3. The Benghazi consulate attack

While running against Obama in the primary, Hillary Clinton's campaign ads inferred that Obama's lack of experience would be a problem if the red emergency phone rang in the wee small hours requiring a decision from him.

I totally agreed with the ad until the part about how she would be experienced and trustworthy in the same situation, because of her eight years experience living in the White House. (Can a doctor's wife perform brain surgery)?

After she lost the election, she changed her mind and became an ardent Obama supporter. Ah politics. All it cost him was a major cabinet appointment. (Secretary of State—that's pretty major).

Into his second term as president, it would seem she was too lenient in her concern in the primary: in light of the vacillating in his "red line crossed" response to Syria's chemical weapon assault on civilians, it appears that it might not matter what time of day the call came.

Then came Russia's attempt to annex Crimea. Putin showed his complete contempt for Obama's warnings. What should Obama do? I don't think he can do anything.

Refer to the assessment of the Afghanistan situation in this book; specifically the story of the aggressive tribal leader's visit to the American construction camp:

"They had apparently crossed the Helmand above and passed in front of the village of Kajakai; four or five men with rifles scorning a full village of armed men. Such is the value of reputation."

The value of reputation works both ways. Obama has lost his in more than four years of scorning our allies, kowtowing to our enemies, and drawing meaningless "red lines to not be crossed."

Most Dangerous

During the 2012 election, I wrote in a blog:

The current President of the United States has campaigned and served based on deceit. Having no record to claim (community organizer and brief state and federal senate seats studded with noncommittal votes of "present") Barack Obama ran on vague promises of "change you can believe in." Voters, unhappy with the then current situation, imagined the changes they wanted to believe and elected him.

How did that turn out? A few examples:

- He promised the most transparent administration in history.

  —He refuses to release his college records—either as student or professor.

  —Major legislation is pushed through without the opportunity for anyone to read the bills' hundreds of pages (not even the legislators who vote on them).

  —When major questions arise as to the actions of the Obama administration (e. g. Operation Fast and Furious) investigators are stone walled.

- He promised to be the President of all Americans.

  —Obama has been totally a party hack. He preaches across the aisle cooperation, but to him that means "agree with me."

  —His Justice Department exists not to serve the people, just the Obama administration's interests.

- He presented himself as a moderate.

  —Barack Obama is the most left leaning President we have ever had.

- He promised that, if his stimulus package were approved, the economy would start to recover.

  —All that has been accomplished is a staggering addition to the national debt.

- He represented himself as outside politics, ready to change the business as usual in Washington.

  —He is a product of the Chicago political machine, and he governs accordingly.

What has Barack Obama accomplished so far in his presidency?

- He has expanded the national debt more than any other president. in history.

- His handling of foreign affairs has diminished America's respect in the world, and has encouraged aggression toward us.

- He has tremendously expanded the size and power of the Federal Government, totally ignoring Constitutional limitations.

- He has also expanded the power of the Executive Branch, bypassing the Legislative Branch, and again totally ignoring Constitutional limitations.

- He has continuously run for reelection.

That last, he has continuously run for reelection, has held back his efforts to subvert the Constitution and remake the United States of America in the European image. (Have you noticed what this has done to the economies of those nations)?

He has held back on some of the most unpopular of his plans for fear of damaging his reelection chances. Can you imagine what he'll do with reelection not an issue? Do you remember his early remarks? Such as: "I won," and "Only the government can..."

> The "Imperial Presidency" will move on with more run away spending, more regulations curtailing business growth, and less regard for the Constitution in a vain attempt to fix the economy.

Was I right in my predictions? Pretty much. Consider that right after winning reelection he: began pursuing gun control, one of his major ambitions that he did little about in his first term (it's a proven vote loser), and increased issuing executive orders creating obstacles to business growth.

When Congress did not support his demands, Obama declared that "I've Got A Pen And I've Got A Phone" and vowed to move forward through executive orders. (Obama is reputed to be a Constitutional scholar. If he has even read that document, he must hold it in contempt).

The Rule Of Law

One of the often criticized characteristics of the Obama administration is his tendency to both ignore existing law and create new "laws" through executive orders. The United States is based on the rule of law, including laws governing the creation of new laws, not the decisions of current officials.

That said, what about laws? Which laws are good and which are bad?

In my book, <u>The Right to Bear Arms and the Wisdom of Doing So</u>, I covered this in some detail. I can't think of anything to add, subtract, or change to that, so I'll include it here as written.

Justification Of Laws

The concept of a free society is that anyone should be free to do anything as long as it does not violate the rights of others. Therefore, any law which forbids anyone from doing anything or requires anyone to do anything is at best a necessary evil.

It follows then that all laws should have demonstrable valuable results or they should not exist.

There is no greater violation of someone's rights than to take his/her life so there is no possible argument against the law forbidding murder. Nor are there any reasonable arguments against laws forbidding taking someone else's property or battering someone's person. Where the gray area begins is with activities which do not violate anyone's rights in and of themselves, but could possibly lead to consequences which would violate someone's rights.

An example of this is driving an automobile at extremely high speeds. The act itself is no harm to others, but can create the danger of having an accident resulting in loss of life or property. Clearly this act is properly controlled by law.

It is obvious that there are two types of actions that are properly controlled by law: 1) those which violate the rights of others, and 2) those which create a risk of something else happening which would violate the rights of others.

In the former case, there is no question. The act should be illegal. The only questions are the severity of penalties and the best methods of enforcement. The latter case involves more questions. To continue with the speeding example, what is too fast?

Forbidding automobile use entirely would completely prevent automobile accidents, but our economy, our culture are dependent on automobile use. A 25 miles per hour speed limit would decrease accidents and lessen their severity when they did happen, but our economy, our way of life depend on rapid transportation. A balance must be achieved between the risks and the advantages of the action.

To do this, a cost benefit analysis is required. For the automobile speed limit, the statistical prediction of accidents at a given speed limit (the cost) is compared to the acceleration of commerce and commuting (a benefit) to determine an acceptable level of the risk. Any law can be judged in the same way: by comparing the risk of allowing an action to the benefits of allowing the same action. If a significant advantage to having the law cannot be shown by this analysis, *the law should not exist.*

Scandals

Earlier I mentioned that immediately after Obama won reelection, problems that would probably have cost him the election had they come out earlier began to emerge—along with the evidence that they had been kept quiet with a series of cover ups.

These scandals include:

1. The IRS attack against conservative political groups

2. The NSA "Big Brother" spying on the American public

3. The Benghazi consulate attack

Added to these are a series of existing and ongoing problems including:

1. Operation Fast and Furious

2. Obamacare

3. Unequal action of Holder's crew

Worsening all of these was the ever present stonewalling of

investigations.

The IRS attack against conservative political groups

The Tea Party was very active in the 2010 election where the Republican Party regained control of the House of Representatives, but was much less of a force in the 2012 presidential election.

The IRS scandal exploded when the Internal Revenue Service admitted in May of 2013 that it had targeted conservative Tea Party groups for extra scrutiny at the time of the election campaigns.

This admission was prompted by the Treasury Department's Inspector General report which stated that the IRS developed "inappropriate criteria" in focusing on conservative groups:

> "The IRS used inappropriate criteria that identified for review Tea Party and other organizations applying for tax-exempt status based upon their names or policy positions instead of indications of potential political campaign intervention. Ineffective management: 1) allowed inappropriate criteria to be developed and stay in place for more than 18 months, 2) resulted in substantial delays in processing certain applications, and 3) allowed unnecessary information requests to be issued."

These inappropriate actions hindered the effected organizations' ability to campaign—possibly significantly influencing the outcome of the election.

The IRS attempted to place the blame on a few "misguided" employees in their Cincinnati office, but it appears that the orders came from much higher up.

Additional complaints have been made by individuals who have been harassed by the IRS apparently because of their political actions and comments.

The head of the IRS department responsible has twice refused to testify on the grounds of self incrimination.

The NSA "Big Brother" spying on the American public

The fact that the National Security Agency (NSA) has been collecting and storing data about U.S. Citizens on a massive scale was revealed when Edward Snowden, a computer specialist who worked for the CIA and then was a contract employee for the NSA, leaked a large volume of classified documents to the media. These documents revealed details of global surveillance programs of an unprecedented scale.

Although ostensibly for tracking terrorists to support national security, this data tracking capability has apparently been used to track governments of friendly nations, used for political purposes, and even to track love interests by NSA employees.

However beneficial for national security, the capability for the NSA to spy on just about anyone it wants to creates a grave danger. In addition to the obvious fear of our government misusing it against private citizens in a 1984 style scenario, the existence of such a massive data base of information presents a target for hackers interested in identity theft and other criminal activity.

In Snowden's words, "There is a huge difference between legal programs, legitimate spying...and these programs of dragnet mass surveillance that put entire populations under an all-seeing eye and save copies forever...These programs were never about terrorism: they're about economic spying, social control, and diplomatic manipulation. They're about power."

Whether you consider Snowden a heroic whistleblower or a criminal and a traitor, the extreme danger he exposed must be judged separately from his action and not ignored.

The Benghazi consulate attack

An armed group of more than 100 terrorists attacked the American diplomatic mission at Benghazi, Libya on the night of September 11, 2012, killing two U.S. Citizens including U.S. Ambassador J. Christopher Stevens.

Early the next morning, a second assault targeted a CIA annex compound about a mile away, killing two embassy security personnel. Ten others were injured in the attacks.

The Obama administration attempted to blame the violence on a spontaneous demonstration brought about by a video offending Muslims—a video that probably never even reached Libya—even though it was later shown that the truth was known even as the falsehood was repeated.

However, with the help of the media, the terrorist nature of the attack was successfully downplayed until after the election (preserving the claim that the war on terror was largely won—a basic Obama campaign boast).

The Secretary of State at the time, Hillary Clinton, nobly claimed responsibility, but ducked testifying by falling on her head and suffering a concussion. She resigned her office after a sufficient time so it would not seem she was quitting over Benghazi, and distanced herself. (The Democrats are doubtlessly hoping to run her in 2016 as "who you really should have elected", the anti Obama. A little hard after she served in Obama's cabinet, but worth a try. Who else do the Democrats have? Joe Biden?).

Many questions remain unanswered: why the ambassador was there in a hazardous area with little protection, why his requests for additional security were not granted, why no attempt was made to send rescue forces (or if too late for rescue, to stomp on the terrorists while they were still there so such attacks would not look so inviting).

As usual in dealing with the "most transparent administration ever" answers disappear in a mass of stonewalling.

Operation Fast and Furious

Operation Fast and Furious was an ATF sting operation *presumably* designed to obtain information about Mexican drug cartels by allowing purchases by gun runners to "walk" across the border to be traced as they were delivered to drug cartels.

It was based on the earlier Operation Wide Receiver, a similar much smaller effort noted for its lack of success. The difference between the two operations, besides size, is that Fast and Furious caused greater carnage, and perhaps wasn't intended as a sting operation at all, but rather to bolster the Obama administration's contention, proved false by the Bureau of Alcohol, Tobacco, Firearms and Explosives (BATFE) statistics, that the majority of guns used in Mexican crimes are from the United States.

To compare the two operations:

According to "A Review of ATF's Operation Fast and Furious and Related Matters" by the U.S. Department of Justice Office of the Inspector General:

Operation Wide Receiver:

1. A total of 474 guns were purchased and 64 were recovered; more than 400 guns were lost track of.

2. A general lack of coordination between involved departments and general insufficiency of supervision prevailed throughout the project.

3. Former Attorney General Mukasey was not briefed about

Operation Wide Receiver or gun "walking." He was briefed only on a different and traditional law enforcement tactic that was employed in a different case.

Operation Fast and Furious:

1. Nearly 2,000 guns were purchased as a result of this operation. The vast majority of these purchases were made by individuals after ATF agents had identified them as suspects.

2. Hundreds of these firearms were recovered in the United States and Mexico.

3. No arrests or indictments were made until it was learned that two weapons found at the scene of Customs and Border Protection Agent Brian Terry's December 14, 2010 murder had been purchased by an Operation Fast and Furious subject who agents had identified in November 2009.

4. The Office of Inspector General's review concluded that the individuals at ATF and the U.S. Attorney's Office responsible for Operation Fast and Furious failed to conduct the investigation with the urgency, oversight, and attention to public safety that was required by an investigation that involved such extraordinary and consequential firearms trafficking activity.

It seems strange that after the poor success of Wide Receiver that a greatly enlarged operation of the same sort would be launched. A great number of firearms were allowed into Mexico without any arrests until Brian Terry's murder forced the issue. It was almost as if the purpose of the operation was to flood Mexico with U. S. firearms.

On multiple occasions Obama has stated that most of the firearms used for violence in Mexico come across the border from the United States (even after BATFE reported that the true number was 17 percent. See my book, The Right to Bear Arms and the wisdom of doing so for details).

Could Operation Fast and Furious have been someone's attempt to "improve the statistics"? We don't know for sure because Obama claimed executive privilege on any communications with the White House concerning the operation, and Attorney General Holder earned himself a contempt of Congress charge by stonewalling.

Obamacare

Obamacare is an attempt at a good thing: affordable health care for everyone. However, it is something that has been attempted many times with a discouraging success rate. This would indicate that it is a difficult task needing skilled, careful development.

Instead, it was developed by incompetent politicians whose entire emphasis was to "Get the law passed before anyone can stop us."

It was voted into law by our elected representatives who were not doing their job. (Voting into law a bill that you have not had the opportunity to read is a massive dereliction of duty worthy of removal from office).

I say incompetence? How's this?

Nancy Pelosi said, "But we have to pass the [health care] bill so that you can find out what is in it."

You pass a bill into law and *then* check what's in it. How incompetent is that?

Then when the law is initiated, the computer system required to enter and maintain the records needed for health insurance policies proves to be riddled with errors. Too many errors to work. A massive push to correct finally gets policies issued, but well behind the number scheduled.

It turns out that all the components of the system were not tested together until about two weeks before launching and that there were errors detected and not yet fixed at initiation.

I know a bit about software testing. I always favored having a test analyst working with the development team testing from a user perspective from day one. In any case, a system this complex should have user perspective testing for a matter of months, not two weeks. *And you don't release a system with uncorrected known errors!*

Okay, so now the system is able to create policies—what about handling claims? An insurance policy with all the required bells and whistles that the government wants is just a useless decoration unless it processes claims efficiently. Will we find the system as "not ready for prime time" in claims processing as it was in policy issuance? History up until now would indicate we will. The push seems to be to get everyone signed up, then we'll worry about how the system works. (Sort of like "...we have to pass the [health care] bill so that you can find out what is in it.")?

Then there are security concerns. Obamacare will create a massive collection of sensitive information on millions of individuals, just ripe for collection by hackers. Such a system requires the ultimate in security. Why should we expect the ultimate in security to be accomplished by a team that had such difficulty with creating a workable data entry system? That's scary.

All right, suppose they get the computer system working like a precision clock; what do we have?

It looks like we'll have a system of healthcare with fewer choices, higher costs, more patients and fewer doctors. And no more people covered, if as many.

Not what we were promised, is it?

Well, Harry Reid assures us that all of the problems we're encountering aren't really true. They are made up and reported by hired actors. The whole thing must be arranged by that "...vast right wing conspiracy," right Harry? Man, we're going to run out of Pinocchios to hand out at this rate.

Unequal action of Holder's crew

One of the foundations on which our country is based is the rule of law rather than arbitrary decisions by those in power. The Constitution of the United States of America was adopted as the basic rule of law, defining the limited authority of the Federal Government, and establishing the Executive, Legislative, and Judicial branches, each with specific authority:

1. The Executive Branch enforces the laws.

2. The Legislative Branch makes the laws.

3. The Judicial Branch sees that the laws and the enforcement of those laws are in agreement with the Constitution.

When the Judicial Branch makes such creative decisions that they essentially create new laws, or the Executive Branch creates new "laws" through executive order ("I have a phone and I have a pen..." Thank you Mr. President), or decides whether or not to enforce particular laws, the system of checks and balances falls apart.

The current Justice Department (led by Eric Holder) is *very selective* as to which laws to enforce and which to not enforce and when to enforce them.

Attorney General Holder is also selective about *obeying* laws.

Selective Enforcement of Laws

Attorney General Holder appears to be a strong believer in all people being equal under the law—just some people are a lot more equal than others.

He has:

1. Filed lawsuits to prevent states from strictly enforcing immigration laws while ignoring states and cities that declare themselves "sanctuaries" for illegal immigrants, in direct violation of Federal laws

2. Sued states to cancel laws against voter fraud.

3. Dropped charges against members of the New Black Panther Party who intimidated white voters in Philadelphia.

4. Ordered ICE agents to not detain illegal aliens who have children.

5. Told state attorneys general that they do not have to enforce the laws that they think might be discriminatory.

6. Did not challenge Washington and Colorado referendums allowing adult recreational use of marijuana although they violate federal law, but fights Texas over voting laws.

7. Refused to acknowledge the existence of the "knockout game" craze, typically done by black attackers, until a white man attacked a black man. Then federal legal action was swift. (The object of the knockout game is to attack a stranger on the street and "knock him out" with a single blow, hopefully recording the act with a cellphone and posting the video online).

8. In hearings before the Senate Judiciary Committee, repeatedly claimed that hate crime laws are designed to protect only groups that were targeted for violence on a "historic basis," such as African-Americans, Hispanics, Jews, and gays. (This puts enforcement of the law out of touch with modern reality. According to the Justice Department's statistics, only 10% of the 650,000 violent interracial crimes that occur each year in this country involve white offenders attacking black victims).

Selective About Obeying Laws

Attorney General Holder is also selective about obeying laws. The law requires that he respond to Congressional committee investigations. His stonewalling (a specialty of the "most transparent in history" Obama administration) caused him to receive the first contempt of congress citation ever issued to a serving cabinet member. I doubt if much will come of that, however. What's the next step? The contempt citation should be prosecuted. Who is supposed to prosecute? Eric Holder's Justice Department. Good luck on that.

BLM invasion of Nevada

The battle between the BLM and a cattle rancher in Clark County Nevada has been going on for years. The rancher's family has been running cattle on the land for well over a hundred years. Apparently he does not recognize the BLM's right to control the land, an attitude prevalent in Nevada. (I learned that when I first moved from California; if you asked if a certain piece of land was BLM land, you were politely corrected, "...it's Nevada open range").

The BLM says that he owes $1.1 million dollars in grazing fees and penalties; he says he owes more like $200,000 dollars and has offered to pay it to Clark County which has not accepted.

Apparently the rancher at one time paid the BLM until they declared the area a protection zone for an endangered species of tortoise and off limits to cattle. At this point, he questioned the BLM's authority over Nevada state land and quit paying. (You can't keep cattle in tortoise territory, but you must keep up your payments for doing so)?

Because of the time involved, it seems the rancher may have "prescriptive rights" to grazing his cattle on the land in question, and that concern may be why the BLM did not simply place a lien on the cattle in the first place, supported by the court orders for the cattle's removal that the BLM already had. That lien might have been rejected in court if the rancher were able to demonstrate prescriptive rights.

For whatever reason, the BLM chose instead to launch what amounted to a federal government invasion of Nevada, complete with helicopters, SWAT teams, and snipers to support contract cowboys who were to remove the cattle.

They were met with volunteer supporters of the rancher's position, some of them in the form of armed militia.

The BLM backed down from the confrontation coincidentally(?) when Harry Reid's involvement with business deals involving potential use of the land surfaced.

Making no judgment on the rancher's position, the BLM's actions were questionable at best. First, the nature of the organization should be considered. The Bureau of Land Management is an agency within the United States Department of the Interior that administers America's public lands. An administrative agency? What is an *administrative agency* doing with a full SWAT team? Individual hand guns for self protection sure, but armor, helicopters, declaring no fly zones? That's police state stuff.

It took J. Edgar Hoover years to get the FBI armed because they were an investigative rather than an enforcement agency, but now public land administrators can field an army.

Goes right along with the Obama administration's selective enforcement of laws: you can't enforce the border, but you can blow a million dollars or so attacking a herd of cattle.

The War Against American Tradition

Every nation has a national tradition. Language, religious beliefs, common law, ethnic customs, written law, literature, music, economic policies, accepted moral behavior, and many other elements comprise this tradition.

A nation's tradition defines the nation. If that tradition is too radically changed, it is no longer the same nation.

The United States of America was founded on:

- Basic Judeo-Christian morality

- Limited government

- Free market economy

- Individual rights

- Individual responsibility

- English common law

- The English language

- The rule of law

- Freedom of religion (no state established religion)

- Freedom of expression

The Constitution of the United States of America was adopted as the basic rule of law, defining the limited authority of the Federal Government, and establishing the Executive, Legislative, and Judicial branches, each with specific authority. (Not rights; only individuals have rights).

The U.S. Constitution also specifically recognized certain individual rights and referred to the existence of others based on common law. *Recognized* not *granted*. These rights were seen to be naturally existing.

Attacks on tradition:

Basic Judeo-Christian morality

The basic Judeo-Christian morality that is traditional in the United States' culture, while based on two related religions, is not dependent on one's religious belief. One does not have to be a Christian or a Jew (or a believer in any religion) to consider murder to be a crime, and the same can be said for any of the Ten Commandments (or the belief in the importance of family. Nor do you need to believe in Jesus Christ to celebrate the national holiday of Christmas).

These concepts derived from religious beliefs have been entrenched in our culture. Because of this, those attacking United States tradition have been described by some as "secular-progressives". They might more accurately be described as "anti-traditionalists".

.

Limited government

The United States Constitution specifically limits the power of the Federal Government both in Article I and in the 10th Amendment. Over the years the reach of the Federal Government has expanded. Under the current administration this expansion has increased dangerously.

Free market economy

The United States of America was created based on a free market economy. It has thrived on this. Lately there has been a trend toward government control of the economy. This is dangerous. Throughout history, free market economies have out performed government controlled markets.

Individual rights

The United States Constitution has a great deal to say about individual rights. No government in history has been conceived with more emphasis on the individual. The Federal Government expansion has oppressed individual rights.

When is Federal Government control right and when is it excessive? Basically, there is a simple answer: when that control provides the greatest support for individual rights, it is right.

When Constitutional amendments were replaced with "creative" judicial decisions (right to privacy?) the government increasingly oppressed individual rights.

Individual responsibility

Along with individual rights comes individual responsibility. The United States economy has historically been based on individual initiative and effort.

It's right for a wealthy nation to provide for those who through physical or mental impairment cannot provide for themselves, or to provide an economic safety net to prevent hard working citizens from losing everything from temporary misfortune. But to provide a welfare system that creates generations of families dependent on government hand outs is unfair both to those dependent individuals and to the workers whose taxes support them. It also spells eventual doom to the national economy.

English common law

The basis for all U.S. law is the Constitution of the United States of

America. Our common law is based on English common law, with Spanish common law and the Napoleonic code influencing in California and Louisiana respectively. The actions of the current administration totally ignore the Constitution and there is pressure to change our laws to match international law and even Islamic Sharia law.

The English language

In the United States one language has traditionally been spoken by all, giving commerce a tremendous advantage. There has been a tendency to require companies to include Spanish instructions on all products. If this is done as a sales incentive, that's fine. When it is done by government decree, the cost hampers the economy.

The rule of law

This administration consistently both ignores existing laws and creates new "laws" through executive orders. The United States is based on the rule of law, including laws governing the creation of new laws, not the decisions of current officials.

Freedom of religion (no state established religion)

This is being interpreted to mean prohibition of the Judeo-Christian influence on our culture. See above.

The 1st Amendment guaranteed no state sponsored and required religion. It did not prohibit any normally accepted practices in government places (such as beginning a meeting with a prayer or having a copy of the Ten Commandments on the wall).

If the current trend continues, the government will essentially establish a state sponsored and required religion: atheism.

Freedom of expression

The 1st Amendment guarantees every citizen the right "... to lay his sentiments, in a decent manner, before the people."

How's that working out? Okay, so long as those sentiments

agree with politically correct thought.

Politically correct thought has the tendency to discourage and to finally forbid any thought that is not politically correct. At this point, we are well into the discourage stage; how much longer before we arrive at the forbid stage? Have we entered the outskirts already?

This brings up the Common Core school curriculum pressed on the states by the federal government. In addition to simplifying the calculation of mathematics by making it more complicated (only in politics is this possible), many of the English tests contain slightly too obvious to be subliminal lessons in political thought.

One such: teaching materials to prepare fifth-graders for these tests require they edit such sentences as "(The president) makes sure the laws of the country are fair," "The wants of an individual are less important than the well-being of the nation" and "the commands of government officials must be obeyed by all."

The stated purpose is to teach children how to streamline bulky writing; I'm sure they are discouraged from making a correction such as: "The Constitution requires the President to enforce the laws created by the legislative branch of the government."

The Danger Of Political Correctness

There are three areas of objection to political correctness:

1. Inconvenience—why change labels that have worked for years

2. Less Usefulness—the old labels worked; the politically correct not so much

3. Politically correct opinions—downright dangerous

Inconvenience—Why Change Labels That Have Worked For Years?

I can best express this by quoting a scene from my novel, <u>Earth Rise.</u>

To set the scene: Ray Taylor PhD, a retired economics professor and cowboy at heart, has gotten involved in a struggle between a shady corporate giant and an alien civilization. He has just discovered that a former colleague of his is the leader of the aliens' "research team" on earth and who now enlists his aid.

"Amazing how much secretaries learn about their bosses' hidden secrets."

"All right, Taylor, so you know who our researcher in New Century is, but isn't the title of secretary rather old fashioned?"

"Administrative Assistant is politically correct. I don't do politically correct. It's American buffalo, not bison, it's American Indian, of which I am one on my father's side, not Native American, and it's secretary. An administrative assistant was someone in training for a junior executive position when I got out of college."

"Taylor, you are a curmudgeon."

"I prefer to think of myself as traditional."

Author's Note: Like Taylor, I am a Cherokee by blood if not by upbringing, and proud of it.

Less Usefulness—The Old Labels Worked; The Politically Correct Not So Much

I worked as a systems analyst during the period when businesses were busy automating their processing. Too often it wasn't realized that you weren't developing a new system; you were changing an existing one. An unplanned system that had developed over time with little documentation, but a system none the less. These "natural" systems were generally not as efficient as they could be with repetitive tasks, *but they worked.* They got the job done.

The initial planned and automated systems, the few that actually worked, were efficient, well thought out and fast, but they always missed this task or that report or produced data too late for one of its very small but vital uses, resulting in many new manual processes being needed to fill in the gaps.

What does this have to do with politically correct terms? Well like the "natural" business systems, the traditional terms have useful meanings no matter how lacking in logic.

As an example look at the term American Indian. The term came from early explorer's confusion as to where they were. Not much logic to it, but it was generally known exactly what it meant: a member of one of the indigenous tribes of North America, the Five Civilized Tribes, the Plains Indians, and so on. It did not mean Central or South American indigenous populations or Eskimos (Inuits).

The term Native American includes all of those. Also, if you apply logic, it should include all of those born in America.

Then there are years of tradition to consider. I can't imagine Nelson Eddie singing "Native American Love Call," nor anyone looking forward to a Native American summer. Or how about a Native American pony?

How about singing "In My Nativeamericana Home"?

To carry this further, how about the Bison Bill wild west circus? Or Bison, New York?

Politically Correct Opinions—Downright Dangerous

Where could politically correct opinions lead? Let's go back to Earth Rise. Taylor, his work done, is riding off.

> His thoughts drifted to the aliens. *They have the complete cradle to grave state provided security—no worries. But also no choices. And the state gets to decide when it's your time for the grave and you go quietly because you've been conditioned to always obey the commands of the Council without question.*

> *Are we headed that way? The conditioning to obey probably started with something akin to "political correctness," and went on from there. "Zero tolerance" of violence could easily become zero tolerance of non-submission. And certainly total disarmament of the population would be necessary. But that led to total disarmament period when one world government was achieved that had the power to control the population through brainwashing from the time of birth. Hasn't brainwashing of school children been suggested as a way to solve our violence problem by an Attorney General?*

The greatest danger of politically correct thought is the tendency to discourage and finally to forbid any thought that is not politically correct. It could even get to the point where a public official's shortcomings cannot be pointed out without causing an accusation of racial bias. Or has that already happened?

Let's Hear It For Patriotism

Patriotism is under fire coming under a lot of disfavor by the one world government liberals. Apparently the 1st Amendment protects flag burning, but some people try to ban flying the flag on your roof because it might offend somebody.

This isn't new; when I was in college, the intellectual crowd (especially the freshmen and sophomores) always snickered at patriotic statements, calling them nationalistic. But it's increasing. We have a President who has spent a lot of his time giving speeches in foreign countries apologizing for the United States of America, and the current administration is full of high powered legal advisers who say that our Constitution should be interpreted to agree with current legal opinions in the rest of the world.

The President has made a speech calling for a new world order where no nation would lead and all would come together.

What's wrong with this trend? Several things:

1. The United States of America is the most successful nation in history.

2. It has provided more freedom and greater prosperity for more people than any country in history.

3. It moved from a minor power to the world leader in four years to save the world from domination in WW II.

4. The United States has always been the first and most generous in response to other countries' disasters.

That's a lot to be proud of.

The concept of one world government is risky in the best of situations. You have all your eggs in one basket.

As an example of the value of a balance of power: when some states oppressed the civil rights of former slaves, the federal government intervened with the 14th Amendment; states are now rising in protest against federal government over reach.

One world government is risky in the best of situations, and this is far from the best of situations.

All countries but the U.S. have moved away from individual freedom and toward the government running everything with disastrous results. The Obama administration is pushing the United States in this same direction toward inevitable failure.

To summarize:

1. There is a lot to be said for the United States of America.

2. There is a lot to fear in a one world government under the best of circumstances.

3. The direction that the world's governments are taking is not creating the best of circumstances.

So let's get back on the track that made the United States of America great, and let's hear it for patriotism.

Governments Have Authority; Only People Have Rights

There is a great deal of discussion about the conflict between the increasing role of the Federal Government and "states rights." This conflict is misstated: *no level of government has rights; only individuals have rights.* Governments only have various levels of *authority* as given to them *by the people.*

The United States Constitution has a great deal to say about individual rights but nothing about Federal Government or states rights. Even the 10th Amendment, often referred to as the "states rights amendment," says:

"The *powers* not delegated to the United States by the Constitution, nor prohibited by it to the States, are reserved to the States respectively, or to the people" (emphasis added).

Powers, not rights. Nowhere does the Constitution of The United States refer to the rights of any form of government; only the rights of individuals.

The Balance Of Power In A Federal Form Of Government

The framers of the Constitution established a federal form of government, balancing power between a central (Federal) government and the various states. The states were existing, functioning governments—each of the original colonies. The Federal government was the new entity, and as such suspect—having the possibility of depriving the people of their rights.

Therefore, the first 10 Amendments were quickly added to the U.S. Constitution to protect individual rights against infringement by the new central government.

After the War Between the States, the 14th Amendment was ratified to apply the Bill of Rights to the states because the southern states were depriving former slaves of their rights as citizens in an effort to return them to de facto slavery.

Shortly after ratification, concerns that it went too far in denying "states rights" caused judicial interpretation to largely gut the 14th Amendment. Then judicial decisions began to slowly "incorporate" the Bill of Rights, one amendment at a time, into the 14th Amendment making them applicable to the states. The latest such incorporation was when the 2nd Amendment, The Right to Bear Arms, was applied to the states.

If you look to the discussions at the time the 14th Amendment was debated (the only legitimate way to interpret the Constitution) it's obvious that the original intention of the 14th Amendment was to apply the *entire* Bill of Rights to the states.

As a further comment on, "the only legitimate way to interpret the Constitution," the Supreme Court provided a magnificent statement on interpreting the Constitution in DC v. Heller:

``A constitutional guarantee subject to future judges' assessments of its usefulness is no constitutional guarantee at all. Constitutional rights are enshrined with the scope they were understood to have when the people adopted them, whether or not future legislatures or (yes) even future judges think that scope too broad."

This statement in DC v. Heller is not a new concept:

"On every question of construction (of the Constitution) let us carry ourselves back to the time when the Constitution was adopted, recollect the spirit manifested in the debates, and instead of trying what meaning may be squeezed out of the text, or invented against it, conform to the probable one in which it was passed." **Thomas Jefferson**

That statement was made in 1823 some decades after the Constitution was ratified and the Bill of Rights added.

The Overreach Of The Federal Government

From about the middle of the 20th century, the Federal Government has increasingly expanded its authority through use of the 14th Amendment, the power granted it by the Constitution to control interstate commerce, and, especially in the Obama administration, out and out disregard of the Constitution. This Federal Government expansion of power has caused some to denounce the 14th Amendment as an attack on "states rights."

When is Federal Government control right and when is it excessive? Basically, there is a simple answer: when that control provides the greatest support for individual rights, it is right.

Remember, no level of government has rights; governments only have authority, and only that authority they have been given by the people. With that authority comes responsibilities, and the most basic of these is the responsibility to protect the individual rights of the people.

So, when the states failed to support the rights of freed slaves, it was right for the Federal Government to step in. When states failed to support the individual right to bear arms, it was right to apply the 2nd Amendment to the states. (After first admitting that it meant what it said in the first place).

With Authority Comes Responsibility

And it works both ways. When the Federal Government fails in its very basic responsibility to defend the United States borders, it is appropriate for the states to use their police powers to protect their citizens from the very real and demonstrable dangers of open borders.

Where Is Our Government Now?

Earlier I wrote, "Barack Obama is the most left leaning President we have ever had". This means that our government must be moving to the left. What does that mean?

Right, Left, Center, Or Tyranny

The Democrats blame a lot of their problems on a "Vast right-wing conspiracy." Political commentators speak of the far left and the far right in politics. Interestingly enough, if you go far enough left, or far enough right you meet. It's called tyranny. (Think left Stalin or Mao, right Adolf Hitler).

It would seem that there is a rather broad road that's safe to travel politically. How do you stay on it? Do you elect only candidates dedicated to staying on that road? Good luck in finding them.

No, some politicians will always continually pull left and some will always continually pull right. The government then goes down the road veering left and right and, hopefully, staying on the highway. The problem comes when the pull gets too steady in one direction for too long a time and the government runs off the road and bogs down.

This is the current condition of the United States federal government. It has gone so far to the left that we're in a ditch. Didn't Margaret Thatcher say that socialism works until you run out of someone else's money?

Well we have, and are borrowing recklessly and creating additional cash with nothing behind it, to fund more government spending to shore up an artificial recovery (which is visible only on Wall Street—can anyone say "Stock Market bubble")?

How Far Left Is The Current U.S. Federal Government?

My political views have always been a little right of center (along with the majority of middle America—according to polls). Recently, I've become a *little* more liberal on social policies. (Not on economics— conservative economics have been proved successful just as liberal economics have been and are being proved a failure).

However, my political views would now qualify me to be a right wing radical. That is how far left we've gone.

In the election where Obama won his first term as President, there was only one Republican in the running: Sarah Palin for Vice President.

John McCain the Republican Presidential candidate? He would be best described as a Harry Truman Democrat.

Barack Obama? A Marxist/Leninist socialist.

Joe Biden? Hard to say, unless he's just Obama's body armor against the possibility of impeachment.

U.S. National Sovereignty

The United States of America is a sovereign nation, founded on law —both written and common—and defined by tradition. One language has traditionally been spoken by all, giving commerce a tremendous advantage.

The basis for all U.S. law is the Constitution of the United States of America. Our common law is based on English common law, with Spanish common law and the Napoleonic code influencing in California and Louisiana respectively.

Our tradition is based on the melding of traditions from the original settlers and later immigrants that formed our population, and developed into a uniquely American culture through our nation's rapid growth in many different directions.

If A Nation's Sovereignty Is Not Protected, That Nation Ceases To Exist

The laws, culture, and borders of a sovereign nation must be defended or the nation ceases to exist.

This is not saying that laws should never change, nor should our culture never be modified by assimilation of the traditions of additional immigrants. Nor is it saying that the borders of our country be closed.

It is saying that our borders need to be secured, not open, and that no one be allowed to enter en masse to replace our culture and laws with theirs.

If A Nation's Citizens Are Subject To Laws Of Another Nation Or Nations Within Their Own Country, That Country Is Not Sovereign

Then there is the "one world government" problem. We are moving toward a one world government. Treaties are being proposed by the United Nations and other organizations that would allow foreign authorities to dictate the actions of American citizens within our own nation.

This has been tried in the past unsuccessfully, but the current administration may well accept such treaties. When you consider the expressed views of many of Obama's appointees, this is quite likely. As one example: Harold Koh, the State Department's legal adviser from 2009 until recently, believes that judges should interpret the Constitution according to other nations' legal "norms," and that the distinctions between U.S. and international law should vanish.

If the growing power of the United States Federal Government threatens the balance between the central government and the states that was incorporated in the Constitution as a guard against tyranny, the movement toward one world government threatens to remove *all* protection against tyranny.

The thought of a one world government presents two areas of concern: 1) by its very nature it places, "all your eggs in one basket," (If the government submits to tyranny, there is no recourse); and 2) most of the world, especially the forces promoting the one world order, is moving away from individual rights.

The Unelected Political Power That Is The Media

It's obvious that the media has a strong effect on the outcome of elections. A September, 2009 poll from Sacred Heart University supports this; nearly nine out of ten (89.3%) of the people polled considered the media a strong factor in electing Barack Obama as President.

The Intended Purpose Of The Media

The Framers of the Constitution were concerned that there be free discourse of ideas from everyone as this was considered necessary for a representative government. Perhaps this is best expressed in an essay written by a Massachusetts anti-federalist in 1787:

> Civil liberty, in all countries, has been promoted by a free discussion of public measures, and the conduct of public men. The FREEDOM OF THE PRESS has, in consequence thereof, been esteemed one of its safeguards. That freedom gives the right, at all times, to every citizen to lay his sentiments, in a decent manner, before the people. -- "John Dewitt"

"For every citizen to lay his sentiments, in a decent manner, before the people." How does the current media live up to that?

Times have changed, and the greater complexity of our nation would make a literal adherence to this ideal difficult (although the advent of the Internet is changing this), but an adherence to the spirit of this idea would require the media to report all views in a fair and balanced manner. Does it?

A Gallup poll released in early October, 2009 shows that about three times as many Americans see the press as liberally biased as opposed to pro-conservative (45% for a liberal bias, 15% for a conservative bias, and, presumably, 40% considering the media reasonably unbiased). Similar polls conducted by Gallup beginning in 2001 show very similar results every year.

When I was young and studying journalism with the intent of a career in that field, all opinion was on the editorial page, or under an individual's byline to indicate that it was opinion. On other pages, under time lines, a strict, "Just the facts, Ma'am," rule was followed. (To quote Sgt. Friday of "Dragnet").

Now opinions are commonly inserted into straight news stories by the mainstream media, generally liberal opinions.

As an aside, "... to lay his sentiments, in a decent manner, before the people." doesn't give much indication that the intent of the 1st Amendment was to protect pornography or flag burning, does it?

The Danger Of A Politically Biased Media

Totally oppressive, tyrannical governments typically have state run media that report the news favorable to the government and "spin" other news to make it favorable or at least less unfavorable. If possible, unfavorable news events are just not reported—just ignored.

Since the public gets most of their information from the news media, a government controlled media controls public opinion.

The United States does not have a government controlled media (except for TV speeches and talk show appearances by Obama, Biden, Reid, Pelosi, et al), but the left leaning "main stream media" reports the news favorable to the current government and "spins" other news to make it favorable or at least less unfavorable, and if possible just doesn't report—just ignores—unfavorable news. So what's the difference?

The Potential Destruction Of An Economic System

The United States of America was created based on a free market economy and individual liberty. It has thrived on these principles. Lately there has been a trend toward government control of both individual actions and of the economy. This is dangerous.

The Advantage Of A Free Market Economy

Throughout history, free market economies have out performed government controlled markets. For an example, you need only look at post World War II Germany. When German reunification occurred, West Germany, with a basically free market system, was prosperous and productive. About the only thing that East Germany, under a Soviet Union influenced government planned economy, had to offer was a large demand for goods and services not previously available.

The Proper Role Of Government In The Economy

Those who oppose a free market system point to the Great Depression and the current economic crisis as arguments against it. What these catastrophes actually show is that:

1. A free market system cannot exist without rules any more than individual liberty can exist without laws.

2. The government's proper role is to make and oversee rules (laws) that keep the market functioning freely.

3. When the government uses its influence to interfere with the market's basic functioning, the free market system ceases to exist to the extent of that interference.

Anarchy cannot exist indefinitely either in a nation or an economy. If there is no government control, the most powerful groups take control and run rough shod over the populace (creating a de facto repressive government).

To prevent this from happening, the government must establish laws and regulations for control, and maintain oversight. These laws and regulations should have demonstrable valuable results or should not exist (see comments on laws above). Deficiencies in this governmental responsibility, especially as regards oversight, contributed greatly to the 2008-2009-2010 (and how much longer?) recession.

Government Interference In The Economy

Another contribution to the latest recession was the government influencing lending institutions to ignore their usual requirements for loans, enabling lower income buyers to become homeowners. This was a noble goal, but no one benefits from being saddled with a loan that he or she can't afford. As long as the housing price boom persisted, this created little problem; when a mortgage became too much to handle, the house could be sold for as much or more than was against it. When the price boom ended and housing prices started down, however, this was no longer possible. The foreclosures that followed accelerated the housing price drop, turning a readjustment into a plunge.

This unwise government interference had caused the free market system to cease functioning to the extent of that interference.

How Did We Get Into This Mess and How Do We Correct It?

What caused the mess?

There are many reasons that we got into the mess we're in, but they are all because we drifted too far left.

In an earlier topic, Right, Left, Center, Or Tyranny, I explained how, if you go far enough left, or far enough right you meet. It's called tyranny (think left Stalin or Mao, right Adolf Hitler), and that there seems to be a rather broad road that's safe to travel politically.

Some politicians will always continually pull left and some will always continually pull right. The best you can hope for is that they balance each other and the government then goes down the road veering left and right and, hopefully, staying on the highway. The problem comes when the pull gets too steady in one direction for too long a time and the government runs off the road and bogs down.

The United States federal government has gone so far to the left that we're in a ditch.

What can we do? In the short term, we have to pull out of the ditch and stop the runaway pull to the left. In the long term, we have to make corrections to our government (largely returns to the original Constitutional principles) to avoid future runaways (*to either the left or the right*).

The immediate action required

In the short term, the 2014 and 2016 elections, we have to face reality: either the Democrats or Republicans will be in charge. A vote for a third party candidate will be a vote for the Democrats.

If the Democrats win, they will take it as an approval of the extreme left policies of the recent past, and we will continue on until the economy crashes (there's little tendency to change "winning" policies).

So, as much as it pains me to say it, vote party not candidate; no matter how good a Democrat might be, if the Democrats control the legislative branch, Nancy Pelosi and Harry Reid will run things (in the next topic, we'll consider changes to ensure that this situation will not exist in the future). So, on these two elections only, vote straight Republican.

*And vote! Y*our right to vote is accompanied by a *responsibility* to vote.

To the person who just said, "I'm tired of voting for the lesser of evils"; so am I, but if you don't vote, you cast a de facto vote for the *greater* evil.

To the person who just said, "I won't vote in case (fill in the blank— whichever candidate) totally blows it, I won't be responsible for helping to put him/her in office"; By not voting you immediately become responsible for helping to elect the other candidate.

To the person who just said, "I won't vote. The candidate who won the primary isn't a real conservative"; he's probably more conservative than his opponent. Besides, remember you don't want to help put Pelosi/Reid in charge.

The point is, for a republic to work, voting is a *duty* as well as a *right* for its citizens. You cannot escape responsibility by not voting. Also, the "My candidate didn't win the primary so I'm not playing any more!" mentality *should have* gone out with grade school.

Okay, that's what the voters should do short term. What about politicians?

They should remember what Ronald Reagan called the Eleventh Commandment, "Thou shalt not speak ill of any fellow Republican."

Well, that might be a little extreme, but the point is to drop the insane battling in primary campaigns. Sure campaign hard, but over major issues that are important and stress what you will do for those issues if elected—not what a dork your opponent is.

To the person who just said, "If you bring out all of the candidate's problems in the primary, you'll have a well 'vetted' candidate and the opposition won't be able to bring out anything new against him/her in the main election"; they won't need to. You'll have done their work for them. Also, how important is it to be well "vetted"? Look at who won the last two presidential elections. Well "vetted"?

So much for the next two elections. The nearest one is months away and the presidential election is well more than two years in the future. We must live under the current situation until after the 2014 election, and the Obama administration until after the 2016 election.

The only thing that can be done is a holding action, using the "purse power" of the House of Representatives. A note here to the Republican leadership: there is nothing wrong with being the "Party of No" if you are saying no to stupidity.

Obama will not change; he thinks he is right. If he tried to change, he couldn't accomplish much. *He has lost the world's respect and with it the ability to lead.* The same thing happened to Jimmy Carter, but fortunately it happened to him at the end of his first term and before the election. We are looking at a long, difficult lame duck period. And a dangerous one ("I have a phone and I have a pen..." Thank you Mr. President).

Three things should be avoided as much as possible during this period:

1. Military engagements: we still have the best fighting forces in the world, but they are hampered by a weak and indecisive Commander in Chief.

2. Any attempt to legalize illegal aliens even if it is accompanied by improved border control. The Obama

administration will not enforce the improved border control, and will push toward citizenship for the aliens. (More voters dependent on the government handouts=more liberal voters. This could lead to a one party system and, eventually, tyranny).

3. Climate control legislation: this is based on fake science and could crash the economy.

One further caution for the Republican leadership: accept and work with the Tea Party, you need them. And for the Tea Party: work with the less conservative Republicans—even the "Rinos". Save your insistence on "real conservatives only" until the clear and present danger is over. (Do you want Reid and/or Pelosi in charge again)?

The long term corrections

When the country is pulled out of the ditch and is back on the highway, it's time to read the Constitution of The United States of America and start following it again to prevent future mishaps.

Virtually all of our problems have resulted from either misinterpreting or ignoring the Constitution.

Rarely have they been from changes made to the Constitution by the amendment process specified by the Constitution itself. Most often they have been made by "creative" judicial decisions.

Problematic Constitutional amendments

Most Constitutional amendments have worked out well. The process of amending the Constitution was deliberately made very difficult. It requires a strong majority spread broadly through the nation over a significant period of time.

However, it has allowed two amendments to pass that should not have (one of which was repealed), one with unintended consequences, and one that didn't go far enough.

The 14th Amendment had an unintended consequence: "anchor babies." It was intended to prevent states from denying full citizenship to all of their residents, and to apply the Bill of Rights to the states;

certainly not to encourage aliens to migrate illegally and establish a hold on residence by procreating an "American citizen." If it weren't for "creative judicial decisions" this would not be a problem. As it is, the amendment needs correction.

Although the 14th Amendment is strongly criticized as having been responsible for Federal Government overreach, it is actually a valuable safeguard when used properly. What is proper use? When individual rights are best upheld, it is right. Remember, only individuals have rights; governments only have authority as given them by a collection of individuals.

The 17th Amendment changed the method of electing United States senators. As originally planned, the U.S. Senate represented the states, while the House of Representatives represented the people at large.

The idea of a bicameral legislature was taken from England; the House of Commons represented the average people and the House of Lords represented the nobility.

Our new nation didn't have a hereditary nobility, but it had a strong concern about the new central government having too much power. So the states were given their own representatives in the government, the Senate, and senators were appointed by the state legislatures.

The 17th Amendment changed this to direct election, by the voters, of U.S. Senators much the same as for Representatives because:

1. There were problems with corruption in the appointing process

2. "Everyone should have a vote"

This change was unwise; it destroyed the basic difference between the two legislatures, so why have two. Besides, everyone did have a vote. You vote for the state legislators who select the senators.

As far as corruption in the process—a look at Harry Reid's last election in Nevada clearly shows that direct election hasn't improved that much.

The 18th Amendment, prohibition, was achieved largely through the political support of organized crime and created a new criminal enterprise. Fortunately it was repealed.

Does this experience indicate that we should legalize drugs? No, it means we should be careful about changing well established tradition with laws.

The 22nd Amendment, term limits for the President. This was an excellent change; it just didn't go far enough. A companion amendment providing term limits for both the House and Senate is desperately needed. More on that below.

"Creative" judicial decisions

There are too many examples of this to list all or even most of them. After the 1960's, Constitutional Amendments essentially ceased, and were replaced with decisions by activist Supreme Court Justices which read into the Constitution rights that were not there.

One example is the Roe v. Wade decision. You simply cannot support finding a right to privacy guaranteed in the Constitution and then implying from that the founders wished to guarantee a woman's right to abortion. (I'm making no judgment on "a woman's right to choose" one way or another; I'm objecting to imagining things in the Constitution that are not there). An Amendment or state laws are the proper places to address this.

Well, maybe you could make such a wild assumption if you accepted Bill Clinton's idea that the Constitution is a growing, changing document.

However, consider this quote from my book, <u>The Right to Bear Arms and the wisdom of doing so</u>:

"...'On every question of construction (of the Constitution) let us carry ourselves back to the time when the Constitution was adopted, recollect the spirit manifested in the debates, and instead of trying what meaning may be squeezed out of the text, or invented against it, conform to the probable one in which it was passed.' **Thomas Jefferson**

"That statement, made in 1823 some decades after the Constitution was ratified and the Bill of Rights added, made sense. Now, more than two hundred years later, it makes even more sense."

So who do you want to believe, Thomas Jefferson or "Slick Willy"?

Government overreach

The United States Constitution specifically limits the power of the Federal Government both in Article I and in the 10th Amendment. Over the years the reach of the Federal Government has expanded. Under the current administration this expansion has increased dangerously.

The Expansion of the Federal Government

The size of the Federal Government started small and grew steadily through the years, with peak periods of growth brought about by the War Between the States and the resulting reconstruction period, the Great Depression, and World War II.

In recent years, the growth accelerated, and then, starting with the first few months of the Obama administration, exploded. Accompanying the expansion of size and cost, which accelerated and then exploded, was a similar expansion, and explosion of the Federal Government's *power*.

That expansion of power was at the expense of both the states' authority and individual rights.

Government interference with individual rights

The 10th Amendment states:

The powers not delegated to the United States by the Constitution, nor prohibited by it to the States, are reserved to the States respectively, or to the people.

The 10th Amendment was obviously intended to protect the balance of power between the states, on one hand, and the central government on the other. This balance is the very basis of the federal form of government. The balance of power between the Federal and State governments, and among the Executive, Legislative, and Judicial branches of the Federal Government constituted a strong safeguard against tyranny incorporated into the structure of the Constitution. This, together with the first 8 Amendments guaranteeing specific individual rights and the **9th** Amendment that alluded to the other rights not specified but secured by common law, provided an emphasis of the individual over the state unprecedented in history.

Federal Government interference with state authority

Again the 10th Amendment was obviously intended to protect the balance of power between the states, on one hand, and the central government on the other, limiting the Federal Government to the powers specified in Article 1 of the Constitution. The 14th Amendment and other civil rights amendments enlarged this somewhat. As stated earlier, when this Federal interference supported individual rights it was okay; for any other reason, it was not.

When necessary to protect a group's voting rights, Federal interference with a state's ability to control voting was right. Continuing control of a specific state well after the immediate problem is over is not. **Interfering with state voter id requirements is never right.**

Neither are "everyone must conform" issues such as Common Core.

Executive and Judicial Branches intruding on the Legislative Branch

The Constitution established the Executive, Legislative, and Judicial branches of the Federal Government, each with specific authority:

1. The Executive Branch enforces the laws.

2. The Legislative Branch makes the laws.

3. The Judicial Branch sees that the laws and the enforcement of those laws are in agreement with the Constitution.

When the Judicial Branch makes such creative decisions that they essentially create new laws, or the Executive Branch creates new "laws" through executive order ("I have a phone and I have a pen..." Thank you Mr. President), or decides whether or not to enforce particular laws, the system of checks and balances falls apart.

The Presidential power of Executive Orders was intended to allow the President to make detailed decisions while enforcing laws made by the Legislative Branch and approved by him. It was not intended to allow him to "go it alone" if the Legislative Branch did not support his programs. (I have a phone and I have a pen so nah, nah, nah).

If my parenthetical statement is disrespectful of the President making him sound juvenile...well it's because he is being juvenile.

And when the most powerful man in the world acts less than presidential, it creates a danger. A clear and present danger.

Specific Changes
Getting back to how do we correct the problem, specifically. I don't pretend to have all of the answers, but here are some suggestions:

Repeal the 17th Amendment
This Amendment changed the method of electing United States senators. As originally planned, the U.S. Senate represented the states, while the House of Representatives represented the people at large.

The idea of a bicameral legislature was taken from England; the House of Commons represented the average people and the House of Lords represented the nobility.

Our new nation didn't have a hereditary nobility, but it had a strong concern about the new central government having too much power. So the states were given their own representatives in the government, the Senate, and Senators were appointed by the state legislatures.

The 17th Amendment changed this to direct election, by the voters, of U.S. Senators much the same as for Representatives.

This change was unwise; it destroyed the basic difference between the two legislatures, so why have two? The change reduced the balance of power between the Federal Government and the states.

Term limits, term limits, term limits

When our government was conceived, there was no intent of it being run by career politicians. It was thought that an individual, successful in the private sector, would seek political office to serve for a few years and then return to the private sector.

Now career politicians are the norm. What makes it worse are those who make a career in the House or Senate winning election after election by providing the voters in their district with favorable representation. (More favorable with each election as they gain influence through the seniority systems of both houses).

Also, Representatives and Senators become more "citizens of Washington DC" and lose contact with reality.

To the person who just said, "If you don't like them vote them out;" I say: Harry Reid's actions effect every U.S. citizen but only the rather small population of the State of Nevada can vote on him.

We need term limits.

Secure the border

We have three problems with our southern border: 1) illegal aliens enter in droves, 2) drug cartels invade and establish surveillance outposts on U.S. Soil to track law enforcement efforts and monitor smugglers around them, 3) Mexican army units enter with impunity and confront U.S. Border Patrol agents (not to mention the possibility of terrorists entering).

Border patrol and state law enforcement agencies in border states are overwhelmed. The task is too large (even if the Federal Government weren't hampering their efforts).

What should we do? What does the Constitution say?

Article IV, Section 4 requires: The United States...shall protect each of them (each state) against Invasion;...

There you go. Take the troops returning from Iraq and Afghanistan and, instead of laying them off and adding to unemployment, place them on our southern border.

The Border Patrol could then competently handle the official entry/exit zones, and the U.S. Army and Air Force could defend our borders as is their job.

You wouldn't have to shoot innocent people attempting to enter or worry about deporting them. *If you have enough soldiers on the border you can just turn them back and when the word gets out they will quit coming.*

The drug cartels? Put out the word that the locations of their surveillance outposts are known, and any movement they make back toward Mexico will not be hindered. Movement in any other direction or failure to move after a specified period and they will be destroyed.

Stop the "anchor baby" madness

The 14th Amendment had an unintended consequence: "anchor babies." It was intended to prevent states from denying full citizenship to all of their residents, and to apply the Bill of Rights to the states; certainly not to encourage aliens to migrate illegally and establish a hold on residence by procreating an "American citizen." If it weren't for "creative judicial decisions" this would not be a problem. As it is, the amendment needs correction.

What is required: either a change to the 14Th Amendment to specify only those born in the United States to a mother *legally* in the country are entitled to citizenship, or a corrected ruling by the Supreme Court based on the intended meaning of the Amendment which would do the same thing.

Reform welfare

It's right for a wealthy nation to provide for those who through physical or mental impairment cannot provide for themselves, or to provide an economic safety net to prevent hard working citizens from losing everything from temporary misfortune. But to provide a welfare system that creates generations of families dependent on government hand outs is unfair both to those dependent individuals and to the workers whose taxes support them. It also spells eventual doom to the national economy.

All capable long term welfare recipients should be required to work (even if it is "makeshift" work). Training should be provided to help them achieve real work, and *welfare recipients should never have a higher standard of living than low income workers.*

To the person who just said I'm cruel, heartless, and unconcerned with the poor; I say: I'm concerned with what will happen to them when the overloaded economy crashes and they lose their hand outs.

Change the organization of both houses of congress

The Constitution pretty well leaves it to the House and Senate to establish their rules of procedure. That's well and good but one thing must change: it's wrong that one person (such as Nancy Pelosi, Harry Reid or, for that matter John Boehner) can prevent a bill from being considered even if it has the votes to pass.

Require laws to comply with the Constitution

Congress should consider the Constitution when introducing bills to be made into laws, asking themselves, "Where in the Constitution are we empowered to do this?"

This seems to be the last thing on their minds. When a journalist asked then Speaker of the House Nancy Pelosi where the U. S. Constitution authorizes congress to order Americans to buy health insurance, Pelosi replied, "Are you serious? Are you serious?" When asked about Pelosi's reply to the question, her press spokesman replied, "You can put this on the record, that is not a serious question. That is not a serious question."

Well, it certainly was a serious question. In a highly political and questionable move the Supreme Court got around that serious question by calling it a tax. (You are required to buy a certain type of policy from an insurance company under penalty of law and that's a tax? Not hardly, Pilgrim).

Limit police powers of Federal agencies

It took J. Edgar Hoover years to get the FBI armed because they were an investigative rather than an enforcement agency, but now public administrators can field an army.

What are *administrative agencies* doing with full SWAT teams? Individual hand guns for self protection sure, but armor, helicopters, declaring no fly zones? Arresting demonstrators? That's police state stuff.

Require that all members of either House or Senate read any bill they vote for

Establish by law that a yes vote for any bill is a statement under oath, punishable for perjury, that the Senator or Representative voting has read the bill.

To the person who just said, "But that would result in fewer and shorter laws;" I say, "That's bad?"

Crush Common Core and any other Federal Government attempts to standardize education

The balance of power between the Federal Government and the states provided by the Constitution totally breaks down if the Feds specify the education of future voters.

Limit Executive Orders

The Presidential power of Executive Orders was intended to allow the President to make detailed decisions while enforcing laws made by the Legislative Branch and approved by him. It was not intended to allow him/her to pass new laws. There should be an after the fact review by the Senate (after it is again controlled by the states) on any executive order to affirm that it is not an overreach. (After the fact to satisfy the need for fast response that is one legitimate purpose of executive orders).

About The Author

Patrick Thomas was born in California and grew up in Massachusetts, North Carolina, Missouri, California, Wyoming, British Columbia, and celebrated his 13th birthday living in a construction camp in Kajakai, Afghanistan.

When not growing up or working in construction camps, he grew up or worked in farming.

After graduating from the University of California with a BA degree in Economics and Political Science, he worked in several industries.

On the side, he served 3 years as a reserve deputy with the Los Angeles County Sheriff's Department, and 5 years with the California National Guard as a Tank Commander and Platoon Sergeant.

After almost 50 years in industry, he retired with his wife of 40 years to northeastern Nevada to use his more than 20 years experience as a technical writer and more than 50 years as a horseman to "train horses and write books."

A Clear and Present Danger
a matter of personal liberty and economic prosperity
is his second non-fiction.
He previously wrote:
The Right to Bear Arms and the wisdom of doing so.

He also wrote two novels:
Shadows of Evil—the vampires among us,
and Earth Rise.

Patrick Thomas' web page is www.wolfeagle2012.com

and he can be contacted by email at wolfeagle@wolfeagle2012.com